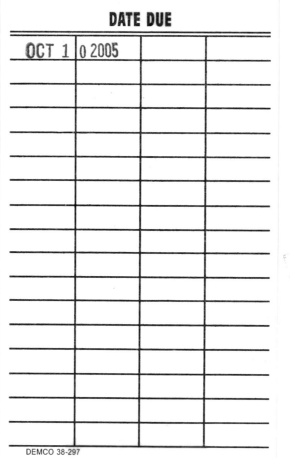

DATE DUE

OCT 1 0 2005			

DEMCO 38-297

CALF TO COW

ANIMALS GROWING UP

Jason Cooper

Rourke

Publishing LLC

Vero Beach, Florida 32964

© 2004 Rourke Publishing LLC

www.rourkepublishing.com

PHOTO CREDITS: All photos © Lynn M. Stone

Title page: *A Dutch belted cow licks its newborn calf.*

Editor: Frank Sloan

Cover design by Nicola Stratford

Library of Congress Cataloging-in-Publication Data

Cooper, Jason, 1942-
  Calf to cow / by Jason Cooper.
    p. cm. — (Animals growing up)
Contents: Cattle — Newborn calves — Calves growing up.
Includes bibliographical references and index.
  ISBN 1-58952-690-2 (hardcover)
  1. Calves—Juvenile literature. 2. Cattle—Juvenile literature. 3.
Cows—Juvenile literature. [1. Cattle. 2. Cows. 3. Animals—Infancy.]
I. Title. II. Series: Cooper, Jason, 1942- Animals growing up.
  SF205.C66 2003
  636.2—dc21
                                                    2003007267

Printed in the USA

CG/CG

Table of Contents

Cattle

    Cattle are big, hoofed animals related to bison and buffalo. There are many kinds, or **breeds**, of **domestic** cattle. But all, like dog breeds, are basically the same animal. Like dog breeds, cattle breeds differ in some ways.

    The colors of each breed may be different. The horns may be different. The body shape may be different. And some breeds are much larger than others.

Most cattle grow horns. Farmers remove the horns of most cattle, but not from the wooly highland breed.

Newborn Calves

With such differences in cattle, no wonder their calves don't look alike! Take size, for example. The newborn calves of large-breed cattle may weigh about 100 pounds (45 kilograms). Newborn calves of small cattle weigh about 50 pounds (23 kilograms).

This newborn Holstein dairy calf weighs nearly 100 pounds (45 kilograms).

Calves, however, are far more alike than they are different. They are born with coats of hair in place. Their eyes are open.

Except for its very long legs, a calf looks much like a small version of its mother. Those long legs are shaky at first, so newborn calves aren't quite ready to run. But they soon stand. And within several hours, a calf can trot after its mother.

Just 12 hours old, this Guernsey dairy calf can already trot short distances.

Like other mammals, cattle produce milk. Calves begin to grow up by drinking milk.

As soon as it can stand, a calf seeks its mother's milk. The calf is not shown where to find milk. It acts from **instinct**. And, also by instinct, the cow stands patiently while its calf **nurses**.

A beef breed, a longhorn cow nurses her calf in a Texas pasture.

A cow usually gives birth to a single calf. The calf grows in its mother's body for about nine months before it is born.

The breeds of cattle used for milk, called dairy cattle, may give birth at any time of year. Meat, or **beef** cattle, calves are usually born in the spring.

Longhorn calves rest in a bed of Texas bluebonnets.

Calves Growing Up

The calves of most dairy cattle don't nurse for long. Dairy farmers separate a calf from the cow within hours of its birth. The farmer feeds the calf milk for about eight weeks. Beef calves are usually left to nurse with their mothers for four or five months.

This Holstein calf will soon be separated from the cow and raised by the farmer.

A farmer begins to feed a dairy calf soft, solid food within a day or two of its birth. Calf food is a mix of grains, sweetened with molasses. After about eight weeks, the farmer removes milk altogether from the calf's diet. When it no longer needs or drinks milk, the calf is **weaned**.

Young female cattle are called **heifers**. Males are bulls. Cattle grow quickly early in life. By the time they are about 18 months old, they have reached much of their adult size. This is the age, too, when many heifers first become **pregnant**.

Holstein heifers graze in a Vermont pasture.

As her body prepares to have a calf, a heifer begins to produce milk. Dairy cows continue to produce milk as long as they continue to have calves.

Cattle continue to grow until they are about three years old. By then, most of them have reached adult height and weight. Most cattle stand 36 to 44 inches (92 to 113 centimeters) tall at the shoulder. They weigh about 900 to 2,000 pounds (409 to 909 kilograms). Bulls are much larger than cows.

Because these Jerseys are pregnant they produce milk.

Most dairy cattle today grow up on a diet of **silage** and grains that the farmer gives them. Some dairy cattle graze on pasture grasses and crops, too. Most beef cattle spend much of their lives grazing on grasslands.

Brown Swiss dairy cattle spend the summer grazing in mountain meadows.

Hereford bulls are bigger, louder, and much more dangerous than cows.

Glossary

beef (BEEF) — the meat of cattle

breeds (BREEDZ) — particular kinds of domestic animals within a larger group of very similar animals, such as the Texas longhorn breed among the cattle group

domestic (deh MES tick) — a tamed animal

heifers (HEF urz) — female cattle before they have a calf

instinct (IN stinkt) — an action or behavior with which an animal is born rather than which it learns

nurses (NURSS ez) — giving mother's milk to offspring, or for offspring to take mother's milk

pregnant (PREG nunt) — the condition in which a mother has a growing baby in her body

silage (SY lij) — chopped up food crops that are stored in silos for animal feed

weaned (WEEND) — to have been broken of the habit of drinking mother's milk

Index

Further Reading

Bell, Rachel. *Cows*. Heinemann Library, 2000
Doyle, Malachy. *Cow*. McElderry Books, 2002
Miller, Sara Swan. *Cows*. Scholastic Library Publishing, 2000

Websites To Visit

www.cyberspaceag.com/beefcattlefacts.html
www.cyberspaceag.com/dairycattlefacts.html

About The Author

Jason Cooper has written several children's books about a variety of topics for Rourke Publishing, including the recent series *Eye to Eye With Big Cats* and *Holiday Celebrations*. Cooper travels widely to gather information for his books. Two of his favorite travel destinations are Alaska and the Far East.